CRAFT ATTACK!

RECYCLING CRAFTS

Annalees Lim

W

FRANKLIN WATTS

LONDON • SYDNEY

First published in 2014 by Franklin Watts

Copyright © 2014 Arcturus Publishing Limited

Franklin Watts
338 Euston Road
London NW1 3BH

Franklin Watts Australia
Level 17/207 Kent Street, Sydney NSW 2000

Produced by Arcturus Publishing Limited,
26/27 Bickels Yard, 151–153 Bermondsey Street, London SE1 3HA

Editors: Joe Harris and Sara Gerlings
Design: Elaine Wilkinson
Cover design: Elaine Wilkinson
Photography: Simon Pask

A CIP catalogue record for this book is available from the British Library.

Dewey Decimal Classification Number 745.5'84
ISBN 978 1 4451 2937 2

Printed in China

Franklin Watts is a division of Hachette Children's Books, an Hachette UK company.

www.hachette.co.uk

SL003838UK
Supplier 03, Date 0114, Print Run 3036

CONTENTS

Crafty Recycling...4

Jam Jar Lanterns...6

Bottle Tops in Bloom...8

Funny Face Vase..10

Stackable Rocket Boxes.......................................12

Beach Hut Pen Pots..14

Bedroom Pinboard..16

Water Bottle Bracelets..18

Scrap Paper Daisy Chain.....................................20

Peacock Bookends..22

Sunny Days Clock..24

Starry Sky Mail Mobile...26

CD Case Photo Frame...28

Plastic Bag Weaving..30

Glossary, Further Reading, Websites and Index ..32

CRAFTY RECYCLING

You don't have to go shopping to fill your home with cool new decorations and handy objects. You can transform unwanted old stuff into all kinds of amazing craft items! All you need is a little imagination.

Going Global

Always remember to 'reduce, re-use and recycle'. By turning old things into useful craft objects, you will be keeping them from going to landfill and helping our planet!

What a Load of Rubbish!

Your home is sure to be full of unwanted objects that could be used in craft projects. Plastic containers are always handy. Scrap paper can be used in many different ways. You could cut up old clothes for textile crafts. Your friends and family will be amazed when you tell them your new craft projects are mostly made from 'junk'!

Pencils and Pens

It's a good idea to have a pot or pencil case full of different pens and pencils. If you're not sure what to get, start with a nice sharp drawing pencil (HB is good), a set of colouring pencils, some felt-tip pens and a black marker.

Scissors

Even though you can tear and rip paper, most of the time you will want to cut crisp lines. Always be careful when using scissors! If you need to cut tougher materials such as plastic, ask an adult to help.

Rulers

Freehand drawing is lots of fun. However, sometimes you need to be a bit more precise. Use a ruler to measure and to draw straight lines.

PVA Glue

A crafts essential! This sticks most things together and can be used to make papier mâché.

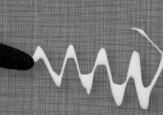

Glue Sticks

These are great for sticking together pieces of paper.

Fabric Glue

This is brilliant for sticking paper or card to (yes, you guessed it!) fabric.

Craft Glue

This is useful if you need to stick metal or plastic things (such as buttons or googly eyes) to your crafts.

JAM JAR LANTERNS

You can easily turn jam jars into beautiful lanterns. They will brighten up any garden, or make a room feel really cosy. The more you make, the better they will look when it gets dark!

You will need
Glass jam jar
Tissue paper
Wire
Wire cutters
Buttons
PVA glue and brush
Tea light and matches

1 Make sure your jam jar is clean. Coat the outside of the jar with a layer of PVA glue.

2 Tear up your tissue paper into small pieces and cover the outside of the jam jar with a layer of tissue paper in a single colour.

3 Cut out leaf shapes from your tissue paper, using scissors. Choose colours that will stand out from your base layer.

4 Coat your jam jar with a layer of PVA glue. Stick the tissue shapes on top. Then coat the whole jar with another layer of glue and let it dry.

5 Ask an adult to cut a 50-cm (20-in) piece of wire and curl the ends so they aren't sharp. Wind it around the top of the jar to make a handle.

6 You will need adult help for this step too. Cut a 15-cm (6-in) piece of wire and thread a few buttons onto it. Attach it to the wire handle and twist the ends again. Finally, put a tea light into the jar and light it.

BOTTLE TOPS IN BLOOM

This fun project will turn plastic bottle tops into flowers that you can use to decorate your room. The best part is that you don't need to water them to keep them looking pretty!

You will need

Bottle tops
Craft foam
Craft glue
Garden canes
Paper
Pen
Scissors
Vase or plastic bottle

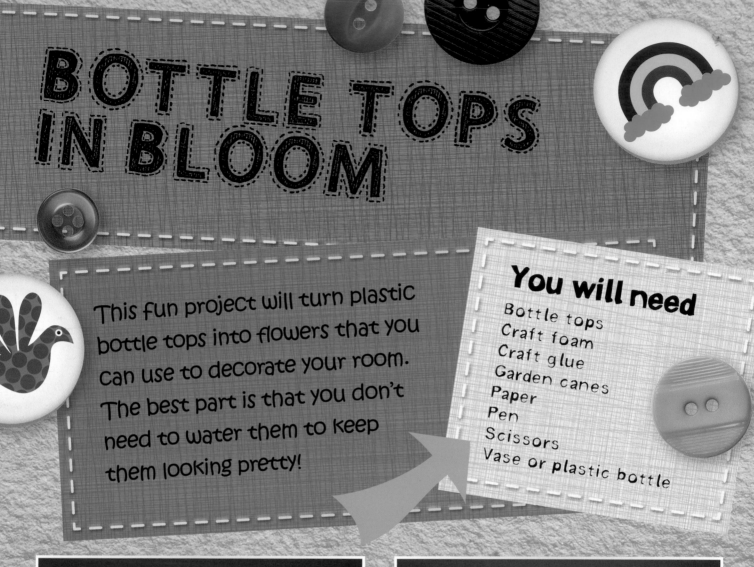

1 Draw a petal shape onto a piece of paper with a pen. Cut it out to make a template.

2 Trace around your template onto craft foam of different colours. Cut out the petals. You will need five petals for each flower.

3 Draw around your bottle top twice onto craft foam and cut it out. You will need two circles for each flower you make.

4 Glue your petals onto the flat part of the bottle top and leave them to dry.

5 Place a garden cane onto the back of the flower and cover it with one of the foam circles, gluing it in place with the craft glue. Turn the flower over and cover the bottle cap with the other foam circle, gluing it down with the craft glue. Repeat steps 3–5 to make more flowers. Leave them to dry, then arrange them in a vase or plastic bottle.

FUNNY FACE VASE

Stop: don't throw away that empty milk bottle! Save it from the bin and make this funky vase. When you put flowers in it, it will look like your crazy character has wild hair.

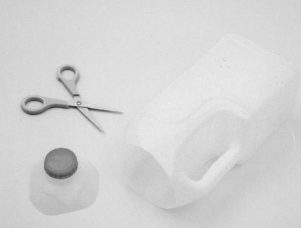

1 Ask an adult to help you cut the top off a plastic milk bottle with a pair of scissors.

2 Draw two small circles (for nostrils), two medium-sized circles (for eyes) and a large circle (for ears) on the card. Cut them out with scissors. Then cut the large circle in half.

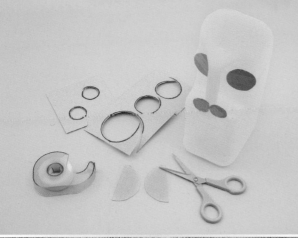

3 Stick the shapes to your bottle with sticky tape, making the handle the nose.

4 Tear small pieces of tissue paper and stick them to the bottle with PVA glue. This is called papier mâché! Keep going until the whole bottle has been covered with paper and glue. Then leave it to dry.

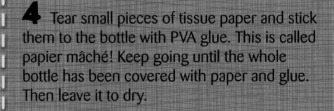

5 Paint it all in a bright colour using acrylic paint.

STACKABLE ROCKET BOXES

These space-themed boxes are made from empty food containers. You can use them to store little objects or hide secret stuff!

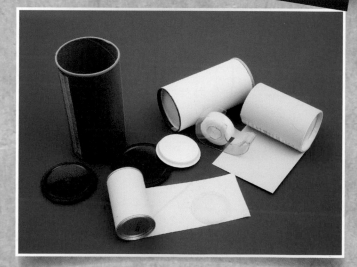

1 Find four tube-shaped containers that will fit neatly inside each other.

2 Measure the height of each tube, and cut a piece of paper to that height. Wrap paper around the tubes and tape it in place.

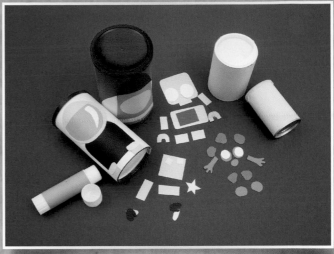

3 Draw the shapes that make up a rocket, an astronaut, a robot and a spotty space alien onto coloured paper. Cut out the paper shapes with scissors.

4 Glue all the paper shapes onto your containers with a glue stick.

5 Outline the decorations with a black marker pen to add some detailing.

Your stackable containers don't need to have a space theme. They can be anything you want them to be.

BEACH HUT PEN POTS

Spending time at the beach is a great thing to do in the summer. With this craft you can still be reminded of those sunny days even when it starts to pour with rain.

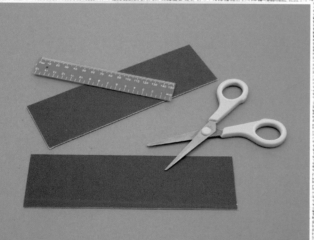

1 Cut a piece of cardboard that measures 6 x 20 cm (2.5 x 8 in).

2 Cut some sandpaper to the same size as your cardboard. Use PVA glue to stick it to the cardboard.

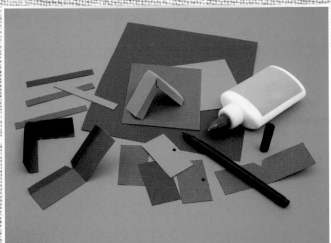

3 Cut each kitchen roll tube in half, to make four tubes. Measure their height and cut four pieces of patterned paper to that height. Wrap the patterned paper around the tubes. Then stick it in place with PVA glue.

4 Cut out four rectangles of card measuring 8 x 3 cm (3 x 1 in). Fold them down the middle, and cut a small notch into that fold. Then fold the edge of the card to the same depth as the notch. Cut four smaller 8 x 6-cm (3 x 2-in) rectangles. Draw on a dot.

5 Glue the card shapes to your tubes with PVA, as shown above. The pointed shapes are roofs, and the rectangles are doors. Glue the beach huts in a row on top of your sandpaper. Leave everything to dry.

BEDROOM PINBOARD

Are you always losing little notes, photos and cards? Then what you need is a personalised pinboard, to keep them all in one place! It's simple to make but looks great.

You will need
Cardboard and paper
Marker pen or pencil
Fabric
Ribbon and buttons
Fabric glue
Large plate
Scissors

1 Draw around a large plate onto your cardboard. Then cut out the circle.

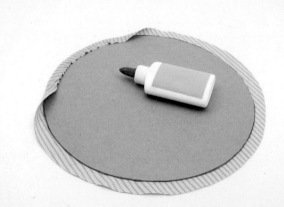

2 Cover the cardboard circle with some fabric. Cut the fabric into a circle a little larger than the plate. Fold over the edge of the fabric and stick it down with fabric glue.

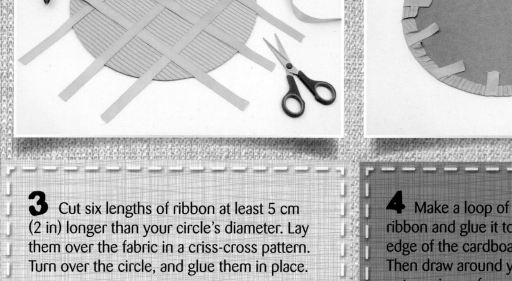

3 Cut six lengths of ribbon at least 5 cm (2 in) longer than your circle's diameter. Lay them over the fabric in a criss-cross pattern. Turn over the circle, and glue them in place.

4 Make a loop of ribbon and glue it to the edge of the cardboard. Then draw around your plate onto a piece of paper and cut out the circle. Glue the paper onto the back of your board.

5 Glue some buttons to the front of your board where the ribbons cross over.

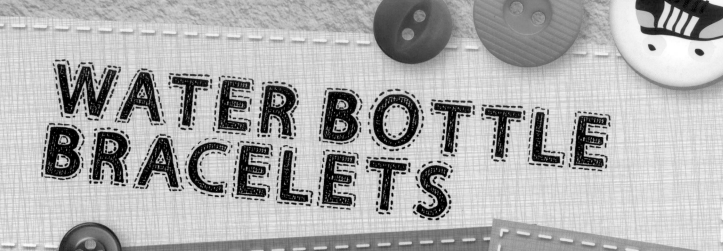

WATER BOTTLE BRACELETS

You wouldn't want to wear jewellery made of junk, right? Wrong! Here is how you can make a brilliant bracelet from an old plastic bottle. It looks anything but rubbish!

You will need

A 2-litre plastic bottle
Wool
Metallic embroidery thread
Sticky tape
Scissors
Black marker pen
Ruler

1 Draw lines around a plastic bottle with a marker pen. Use a ruler to measure them – they should be about 3 cm (1 in) apart.

2 Cut along the lines to make plastic rings. These will be your bracelets!

3 Tape over the edges of each bracelet with some sticky tape, so they are not sharp.

4 Wrap wool round and round each plastic bracelet. Change colours to make stripes. When you're done, make a knot.

5 As a finishing touch, wind some metallic embroidery thread around each bracelet in a zig-zag.

You could also make some smaller rings from a smaller plastic bottle and attach them to a necklace or earring clips!

SCRAP PAPER DAISY CHAIN

Rescue some paper from the bin or recycling box, and you can make a daisy chain that lasts forever! If you don't have a shredder, just use scissors.

You will need
Shredder or scissors, ruler and pen
Scrap paper
PVA glue
Green string or wool

1 Either shred some white and yellow paper, or use a ruler, pen and scissors to cut it into long, straight strips. You will need 10 strips of yellow paper and 60 strips of white paper.

2 Coil the yellow paper into tight rings. Fix the ends in place with some PVA glue. These rings will be the centres of your daisies.

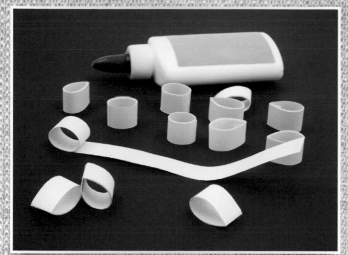

3 Now coil up the white paper into slightly larger rings. Fix the ends in place with some glue. Pinch one end of each white ring to make a point. These will make your petals.

4 Fix six white petals to each yellow ring with PVA glue. Leave them to dry on a protected surface.

5 Peel off the flowers and thread them onto a length of green string or wool.

Make lots of different coloured flowers using shredded magazines. You can use them to decorate picture frames, blank cards or even a keepsake box.

PEACOCK BOOKENDS

If you enjoy making these peacocks, you could also try decorating bookends as lighthouses, moon rockets or the turrets of a castle.

You'll be as proud as a peacock when you show everyone this fun craft. You can use these bird-brained buddies to prop up your books, or as a decoration.

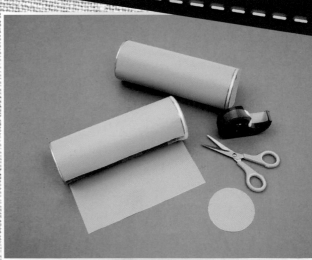

1 Fill two crisp tubes with sand to make them heavy. Replace the lids and fix them in place with sticky tape.

2 Measure the height of your tubes. Cut two pieces of blue card to that height. Wrap them around the tubes and tape them in place with double-sided tape.

3 Draw two body shapes like pinched ovals onto blue card, and triangular beaks onto yellow card. Cut them out and fix them to the tubes with double-sided sticky tape. Then stick on googly eyes with PVA glue.

4 Cut out feather shapes from green, blue and purple card. Stick the feathers to your tube in a fan shape.

SUNNY DAYS CLOCK

You should always make time for craft... and now you can use craft to make a timepiece! The rays of this cheery sunburst clock are made from scrap paper – or you could use newspaper.

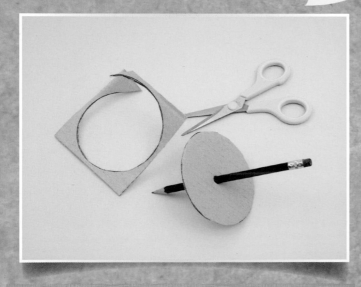

1 Draw around a large cup onto cardboard. Make a hole in the middle with a pencil so that your clock pieces can fit through.

2 Spread some glue down one of the short edges of a piece of paper. Place your knitting needle at the opposite end and start rolling it up into a tube. Fix it in place with more glue. Repeat this 11 times.

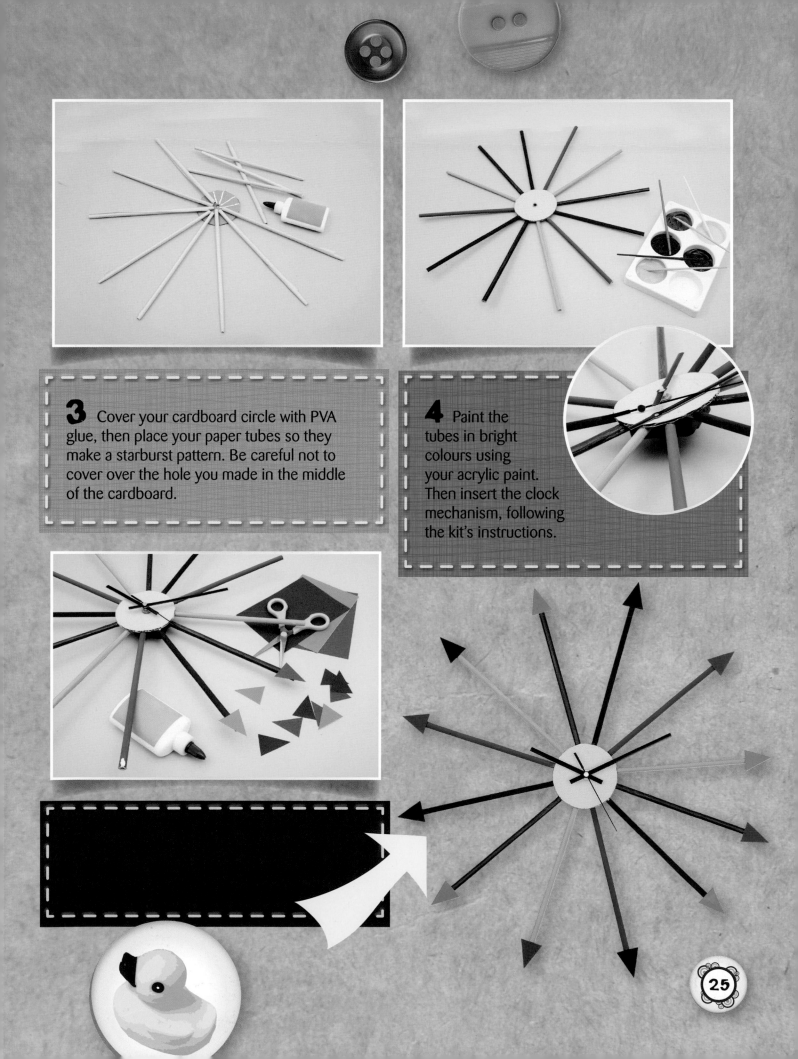

3 Cover your cardboard circle with PVA glue, then place your paper tubes so they make a starburst pattern. Be careful not to cover over the hole you made in the middle of the cardboard.

4 Paint the tubes in bright colours using your acrylic paint. Then insert the clock mechanism, following the kit's instructions.

STARRY SKY MAIL MOBILE

Everyone loves receiving letters, but we usually just put the envelopes in the bin. Why not use them to make a fun mobile? Ask an adult to help with the last two steps.

You will need

- Wire
- Acrylic beads
- Envelopes
- Wire cutters
- Scissors
- Needle and thread
- Acrylic paint

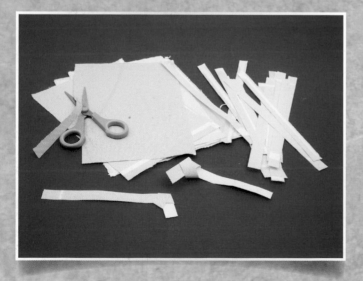

1 Cut your envelopes into long strips, about 3 cm (1 in) wide. Tie a knot in each strip.

2 Squash down each knot, to make a pentagon shape. Wrap the rest of the paper strip around the pentagon and tuck the end into one of the folds.

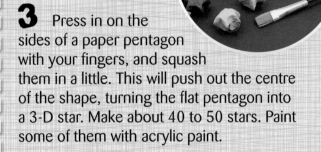

3 Press in on the sides of a paper pentagon with your fingers, and squash them in a little. This will push out the centre of the shape, turning the flat pentagon into a 3-D star. Make about 40 to 50 stars. Paint some of them with acrylic paint.

4 Ask an adult to make a spiral out of wire. Thread the beads onto the wire and curl in either end of the wire to make sure the beads don't slide off.

5 You will need some more adult help with this step. Thread a needle, and push it through five stars in a row to link them together. Tie a knot at the end of the thread and cut it off with scissors. Make at least six starry chains, and tie them to the wire. Then add a loop of thread to the centre of the spiral for hanging it up.

CD CASE PHOTO FRAME

Most people have some old, unwanted CDs at home. Don't throw them out just yet – you can use the cases to make snazzy photo frames!

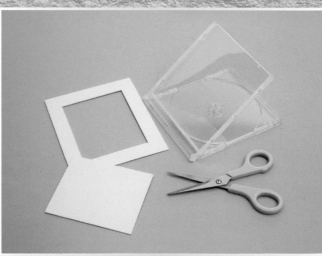

2 Measure, draw and cut out a card frame the same size as your CD case. It should be 2 cm (0.8 in) wide around the rim.

3 Cut some strips of felt about 1 cm (0.4 in) wide and 26 cm (10 in) long. You will need about 36 strips in different colours.

4 Put two different-coloured strips of felt together and roll them up. Glue the ends down so that the coil doesn't unravel.

5 Glue the felt coils to the card and leave to dry. Then glue the card onto the CD case on three sides. Leave one side open so you can insert a photograph.

PLASTIC BAG WEAVING

Every household seems to have a drawer or cupboard bursting with plastic bags – they get everywhere! By weaving several bags together, you can make this cute, colourful pencil case.

You will need

1 Cut a piece of cardboard into a rectangle that measures 10 x 20 cm (4 x 8 in). Snip five small triangles into each of the short sides.

2 Cut the plastic bags into 1-cm- (0.4-in-) wide pieces, so you have strips ready to weave with.

3 Wind strips around the grooves in the card so that you make lines of colour. Fix them in place with sticky tape.

4 Use different coloured strips of plastic bag to weave in and out of the longer pieces. You will end up with a colourful checkerboard effect.

5 Cut the weaving off the board, making sure it doesn't unravel. Fold over the loose edges to make a rectangle and fix it in place with your sticky tape. Repeat steps 2-5 so that you have two woven rectangles. Use more tape to attach the two pieces together on three sides. This will make your handy pencil case.

You could also make a pouch for your mobile phone or music player. Just change the size of the cardboard in step 1 to make the case smaller.

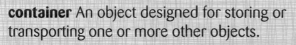

GLOSSARY

container An object designed for storing or transporting one or more other objects.

freehand Drawn by hand, without using guiding tools such as rulers.

landfill The disposal of waste by burying.

papier mâché A hard material made by layering paper and glue.

tea light A small candle in a metal case.

template An object that can be copied.

turret A small tower attached to a larger tower.

FURTHER READING

The Art of Recycling by Laura C Martin (Storey Books, 2004)

Eco-Friendly Crafting with Kids by Kate Lilley (Ryland, Peters and Small, 2012)

Green Crafts for Children by Emma Hardy (CICO Books, 2011)

What Shall We Do Today? by Catherine Woram (Ryland, Peters and Small, 2009)

WEBSITES

kids.nationalgeographic.co.uk/kids/activities/crafts/
Crafts inspired by nature.

www.freekidscrafts.com/recycled_crafts-t27.html
Loads of ideas for recycled crafts.

www.kinderart.com/index.html
Art projects categorised by theme and age.

INDEX

birds 22–23
bottles 10–11, 18–19
bottle tops 8–9
boxes 12–13
bracelets 18–19
buttons 6–7, 16–17

card 10–11, 14–15, 22–23, 24–25, 28–29
cardboard 12–13, 14–15, 16–17, 24–25, 30–31

clocks 24–25

fabric 16–17
flowers 6–7, 8–9, 20–21
foam 8–9

jars 6–7

lanterns 6–7
leaves 6–7

papier mâché 10–11
photo frames 28–29

plastic bags 30–31
pots 14–15

ribbons 16–17

sandpaper 14–15
stars 26–27

tissue paper 6–7, 10–11

wire 6–7, 26–27
wool 18–19, 20–21

SERIES CONTENTS

Jewellery Crafts

Make Your Own Jewellery • Pendant Necklace • Lucky Rabbit Earrings • Brilliant Bead Bracelet • Knotted Bracelet • Cool Collar Necklace • Fabric Flower Ring • Friends Forever Necklaces • Sew Easy Felt Brooch • Funky Toy Hair Clips • Jewelled Cuff • Puzzle Piece Hair Comb • Button Bag Charm • Jewellery Tree

Nature Crafts

Going Wild with Nature Crafts • Woodland Photo Frame • Painted Pebble Plant Pot • Butterfly Bunting • Sand Art • Shell Creature Fridge Magnets • Pressed Flower Coasters • Leafy Bird Mobile • Seed Mosaic • Japanese Blossom Tree • Pebble Zoo • Brilliant Bird Box • Pine Cone Field Mouse • Lavender Hand Warmers

Paper Crafts

Getting Crafty with Paper • Cube Puzzle • Pop-Up Painting • Paper Planets • Paper Pulp Monsters • Make Your Own Notebook • Secret Seashell Storage Box • 3-D Photo Art • Quilling Cards • Giant Crayons • Paper Globe Lampshade • Paper Cup Disco Ball • Envelopes and Notepaper • Paper Bouquet

Printing Crafts

Perfect Printing • Apple Print Canvas Bag • Block Printed Cards • One-Off Portrait Print • Funky Pattern Prints • Stencil Art Plant Pot • Clay Printing • Roller Print Folders • Cling Film Wrapping Paper • Button Print Trainers • Easy Screen Prints • Spotty Painted Mugs • Bubble Print T-Shirt • Sandpaper Printing

Recycling Crafts

Crafty Recycling • Jam Jar Lanterns • Bottle Tops in Bloom • Funny Face Vase • Stackable Rocket Boxes • Beach Hut Pen Pots • Bedroom Pinboard • Water Bottle Bracelets • Scrap Paper Daisy Chain • Peacock Bookends • Sunny Days Clock • Starry Sky Mail Mobile • CD Case Photo Frame • Plastic Bag Weaving

Textile Crafts

Terrific Textiles • Cute Sock Owls • Rock Star Rag Doll • Toadstool Doorstop • Funky Felt Friend • Cocoa Cosy • Totally Brilliant Tote • Awesome Accessories • Jean Genius Desk Mascot • Secret Diary Cover • Mini Bag Organizer • Cupcake Pincushion • Knitted Phone Case